The Face of It

R.F. Langley was born in Rugby in 1938. He was educated at Jesus College, Cambridge, and went on to teach English and Art History in three secondary schools in the Midlands. When he retired in 1999 he moved, with his wife Barbara, to Suffolk, a county they already knew very well, close to the sea, where the natural history is rich, the buildings often fine, and collections of the Norwich School of painters are nearby. So, too, is Cambridge, where much of what he did not find out when being educated there is still around to be discovered, and where most friends are living. Burgundy and northern Italy are also significant places for his writing. R.F. Langley's *Collected Poems* (2000) was shortlisted for the Whitbread Prize for Poetry.

T0099470

Also by R.F. Langley

Collected Poems (Carcanet Press/Infernal Methods, 2000)
More or Less (The Many Press, 2002)
Twine (Landfill Press, 2004)
Journals (Shearsman Books, 2006)

R.F. LANGLEY

The Face of It

CARCANET

First published in Great Britain in 2007 by
Carcanet Press Limited
Alliance House
Cross Street
Manchester M2 7AQ

A CIP catalogue record for this book is available from the British Library
ISBN 978 1 85754 900 3

The publisher acknowledges financial assistance from Arts Council England

Typeset by XL Publishing Services, Tiverton
Printed and bound in England by SRP Ltd, Exeter

Contents

Acknowledgements

'Cakes and Ale', 'Cook Ting', 'Experiment with a Hand Lens', 'Sixpence a Day', 'Still Life with Wineglass', 'No Great Shakes' and 'After the Funeral' were published in *More or Less* (The Many Press, 2002).

'Depending on the Weather' and 'Blues for Titania' were published in *Twine* (Landfill, 2004).

'Cash Point', Skrymir's Glove', 'At Sotterley', 'Still Life with Wineglass', 'Blues for Titania' and 'The Bellini in San Giovanni Crisostomo' were first published in the *London Review of Books*. 'My Moth: My Song', 'Touchstone', 'Brute Conflict' and 'Birdwatching Poem' were first published in *PN Review*.

Cakes and Ale

This bit again. You know it.
It's the sequence in the bar
on an outer planet. You
see piecemeal through the ruddy
strobes and smoke. You must be by
the door, and going through the
motions, brushing off the rain.
Their backs are to you. Hunchbacks.
Some of them wear metal. Fanged
pauldrons, bizarre combs frizz up

against the strip light further
in. Barbarians. Or a
culture in elaborate
decline. Flagrant. Capricious.
You ought to recognise which
tribe. Those red plush tippets. An
occasional glimmer of
a souveraigne collar, if
you're right. Some Gothic warriors.
Braggarde and dangerous. They

have not yet looked round. One turns
to speak. And now you see his
beak and thin, uncurling tongue.
The customers are monsters.
The customers are monsters.
From deeper down somewhere, some
instruments like soft trombones
start blowing a blue hockett.
The customers are monsters.
They have not seen you yet, but,

when they do, they'll love you limb
from limb. Meanwhile they face the
wonderful barmaid, who is
all their mothers still. She gains
her glory nobly tugging
every polished handle in
the middle of her rosy,
pumping heart. They need their nips
of sack and sugar poured by
this real lady, level to

the lips of their own greedy
brimmers. Now she'll look up and
see that you have come, in your
perversity, her erstwhile
son, through the tempest, on the
last night when it could be done,
to the back door, for, once more,
a sop, a sip. Only your
haggard stare can win her. No
secret wink gets you this drink.

Nor the guts to shove you to
the front, as you hold out your
father's empty bag. This bit.
Again. The hockett stops. The
strobes lock rigid at the top
of nightmare. Then a dragon
starts to swivel in his chair.
The barmaid's million hands
close on this one pump handle
and become a simple pair.

Cook Ting

Circumstances analogous
to life and death, house cleaning or
clutter. Dante or an old shirt.
It's there to cut, but not to chop.
Between the knuckle-bones it's soft
as butter. Or you picked a leaf
off the road. What is it when it
reaches the sea? The gulls are a
white flap over sprats in the foam.
Call it an episode when they
tumble together to make it
one. The cliff is history. You
throw yourself in where the fish are
thickest. Take hold of a word and
turn it on. Tourbillion. A
blade is so sharp it can dance round
the joint. Silvery energies
argue the point. The carcase of
an ox flops open. Shall we leave
it at that? Some of the cliff calves
flat. The rest ducks, and runs like a
rat. Look about and wipe the knife.
But there's more, there's more. Rubbing it
out will prove there's no nub of the
matter. There are too many eyes
for your own eyes to catch in the
scatter. Twelve blank sheets of paper
hung up on a string. The joy of
perpetual bicker. Your seat
at the open door. The shutters
banged back. A dark acrobat who
somersaults through to rob a few
of the glittering company.
Is there a wife for a Viking?
A pair of socks in a poem?
Beetles and sticks in a box? Bright
bait. Bright bait. You notice what has
gone into the picture. Bite it.
It can't be expected to wait.

Experiment with a Hand Lens

The clown under
cover. Among
a lot less. Aghast

at much more. A
set of tucked legs,
curled up from

before. His mother's
bug. Her summer's
boy. A bead

she polished first
to put deliberately
last. Her lonely

coal. Kick start.
Heart prick. Fire
crumb. Come close

in focus. Here you
are. The cavern fits
the wren. Lenticular.

This is her son. Her
pearl in the pout. The
merry meal in her

floury mouth. And
so and so. Amen.
But ahoy you young

lout! Not so far!
Not so fast! You
can never tell when,

with that hole in you.
Nothing is less than
particular.

Sixpence a Day

The sea bulges or licks.
Cool as a lemonade.
A gull rides with its two
red feet, dib dab, beneath,
doing appropriate kicks.

So easily can the
low sun rearrange some
pegs, making another
countenance with its legs.
It switches hips, turns on

a toe. Marram shoves its
stems through silica and
an unidentified
spider starts to chew his
gloves. Now here he is, cream

spots on cinnamon. His
camouflage first becomes
his normal wardrobe, then –
Voilà! He's ablaze with
all his badges! Handsome

patches double on his
abdomen. You see the
sense of this, compared with
the mad quarrels in the
mix of flints. Bunch or run,

whatever he does is
excellently done. Gems
will be known and numbered
in the movement of the
secretary's watch. You

rip so you can match. A
nib makes flourishes with
an emphatic scratch. Where
nothing bothered any
more, draught boils a cobweb.

Forgotten by the world,
odd glossy bits blow round,
hang out, shake up. As keen
as mustard every seed
spits on his neaf. There seems

to be no limit to
the amount of life it
would be good to have, just
fingering the thickness
of a leaf. So what if

there are really no grand
narratives? Electric
peaseblossom flutters in
the surf on autumn nights.
Your rapier can still

spear the eel. It can pick
off this particular
caterpillar with a
flick. Your brain finds much to
amuse it in a bush.

You're the best friend of a
naturalist who hugged
himself, expecting it
to be a bear. Stand back.
Give it a chance to growl,

if it is there. The gull
glows. Dusk adjusts its grey
to that. Pit pat. There must
be huge commotion when
you touch shocks of grass. Eight

eyes. Brightest the golden
pair. A clink of chitin
as eight knees slightly clench.
This heartbeat underneath
this cardiac mark, like

a soft pulsation in
a trench. It creaks in the
thicket. Come quick! The room
is full of them, as big
as birds! The great mounsieurs

in white neckties and with
their wings as floppy as
a melancholic's hat.
They hood and wink until
they eventually

clip the little ticket
which is shivering in
the muscle of your cheek.
Don't be dismayed. It's nine
o'clock. Lay all the stuff

you have collected on
the mat. Count the score. Do
the job slowly. Do it
well. Colour them in. Both
flick and flack. Maroon. Brown.

Ivory black. Once you've
got started, most of the
males will stop their flap to
settle down together
round the female on the

bell. O Peter Quince, it's
not knavery at all!
Cool as a lemonade.
The convenient place.
Just as you said before.

Still Life with Wineglass

A wineglass of water on
the windowsill where it will
catch the light. Now be quiet
while I think. And groan. And blink.

I am anxious about the
wineglass. It's an expert at
staying awake. How can it
ever close its eyes? It's too
good a defence against an
easy sleep under the trees.

The wineglass stands fast in a
gale of sunlight, where there is
one undamaged thistle seed
caught on its rim, moving its
long filaments through blue to
orange, slowly exploring
the glorious furniture.

Old Harry has opened that
bundle again. Oh well. Tuck
up your golden sleeves. Fetch out
the white gloves. We'll go right through
the thistle seeds till we find
Jenny.

       The finch's mother
told him about teasels. He
consults them daily with fierce
resignation. His findings,
however, fluff out and cream
off, catching the drift.

Mum was
the word, but she did give a
nod. So they sidled up close,
put a foot on its neck and
kiss, kiss; kiss, kiss. Sometimes they
stopped pecking to watch what they
could not follow. Parachutes
whispering away

Milk and
magenta. A gob of the
cotton, torn from the button,
thrown into despair. So there's
nothing remains of what we
see? Does it? Does it? Tumbled
about in the air?

We speak
from out there and we keep things
alive. The wineglass reminds
me of wading birds, when their
beaks meet their beaks as they feed
on a mirror of mud and
mark 'Here' as a point in the
water that's deep in the sky.

Fetch me a folding chair. Set
it up by the south door. This
is etiquette. I am the
ticket collector. Nothing
comes in but thistledown which
scarcely touches the floor and
was never supposed to pay.

New pennies. Spun into the
droning paternoster. How
close Jenny rose to the top.
Then turned back, and you lost her.

Each bubble considered the
rest as it chose its place. Out
in the morning everything
settled, before I could look.
Down centre is a tomb or
shrine. The sun is shining on
the corner of a panel
set into its side. It's all
paid on the nail. None of it
is mine. Way off, and running
strongly through the hazy, slate
blue sky, that must be rosy
Mercury, bent on a quest.

He did choose the third sister.
Jenny wasn't there. Recent
incidents are never seen
in the crystal ball. Only
a procession of distant
people, passing below a
ruined wall, brightly lit, but
microscopically small.

Soft pappus strings out like a
search party. It's looking for
the concealed figure of a
god. Whoever dropped him in
the clump of weeds forgot him,
so they could seek him in the
sacred hunt. Remember how
the wineglass put its foot down,
chip-chop, happy to be home.

Next. Invent a religious
uncle. He was the one who
taught you elocution when
you lived in the forest. Give
me the details. I want your
whole story clear in my mind.
Rabbits are kindling in their
burrows. Tomorrow Harry
will meet Nuncle just as you
described him. They will sit down
together in the sun and
puff at the dandelion.

A bumper. Little fingers
that were hidden flicked the dice.
The cunning rascals counted
on convincing you these were
the lucky accidents of
a busy day, set, at the
end of it, in solid ice.

The window. The wineglass. A
yew tree inside it, upside
down, far away and very
distinct. A cautious chaffinch
sits tight through the shift of the
consonants. The needles are
green. The bird knows it is pink.

No Great Shakes

Outside, the cones in the pines
are rows of turbines set into
the wind. But, inside, the mind
expects a blow.

Outside, each cone screws into
the wind by a twist of its
scales, up to its head. In here,
there is no thread.

Outside, each bit of twirling
pollen has the best shape for
the flow through the vanes of the
cone. Inside – none.

Outside, the twitchy stems of
grasses make quick snatches in
the air that passes. Others,
stiffer, with a

down-wind bluster, bounce the dust
till time enough for clustered
flowers to catch it. Here, the
mind can't match it.

I cannot tell. Get thee back
into deaf John's dark house. The
draught is trapped and whipped about
the wrist and strapped

so the cold fist warms somewhat
the fingers curling on the
palm. Four worn Jacks turn churlish
in the shaking

hand, grinding uneven teeth.
The same star still burns westward
from the pole. Cock all, I say.
Inside blown out

and topsides down. The clown's own
knuckles are the bones he's thrown.

After the Funeral

In the Ceramic Gallery. No train
till half past five. Yellow.

No amber. A hornet
would be something from another poem,
eager for nectar. We

fleer with yellow leaves. A
row of white bowls that make
mouths at it, months of it,
moon after moon. Colder
and rimmed with copper. In

the Ceramic Gallery, the yellow
October plane tree leaves in Gordon Square.
Nothing slabbered about Pauline's death. Some
details will rustle about or hump it
and call it a sixpenny jug. Think it
as leaves. Think it as bowls. It's a question

of leaves at the top of
their swell, which speak out in
a screed round the scope of
themselves, to die down in
the bowl. Stop. So that they
settle. Or stump up at
once. A hornet could bring
a formidable hum
to the poem. It's the
right time of year. There were
none at the Hampstead Free
Hospital. Nor here. Give

some mind to an empty dish. How, in the
Ceramic Gallery, metal lips fit.
Her passport photograph looks like the moon
in a tight woollen hat. She had given

her money away. Her
stare will say nothing of
that. I forget what is
left of the leaves. But it's
a knuckle keeps rapping
the bowl, so that it rings.
So that it rings and rings.

Depending on the Weather

The hurry to bite that runs over the spare
text, with his head high, with his bulging eyes. He
swerves with the weave, expecting his next success.
Premise:– the beetle believes that he knows what
the wasp is thinking. The beetle believes he
knows what the wasp is thinking of him, the green
beetle, what she sees he might mean, his needles
winking and the wicked cut of his jaws. The
beetle believes he knows what the wasp thinks the
beetle is thinking. About them both. All their
embroidery. His nip. His stitch. The set of
grapples in his grin. The rich twist of his you.
His green me. Two to embrace. Then the toils we
intended to trace. The last clasp. About how
clever to run through what needs must be done, to
be stitched up as them, as the beetle and wasp,
woven deep in and ready to work. But what
we remember, both, as anyone should, is
this shock of this buzz of these silvery wings.

The classic malevolence of the evil
fairy, or your own ill-treatment of the poor.
She passed by the door, speaking nothing. Then she
instantly returned with a like look, and in
the same silence departed. The new wheat-cake
I was chewing fell from my mouth. Myself in
a trembling. Myself off my stool, sewed in a
stocking. Stuck in my fit. I believe the old
widow knew well enough what went right to my
heart. What I ought with my cake. For the sake of
a silent rebuke. My neighbour, the witch, who
is after my cookies. Eye on me, as if
she were Atropos. Green as a beetle that
studies to bite through these golden curls. The twirls
of a wasp round a hot pocket of sand, as
if it were checking its property, combing
out honey. The kingdom of spin and snip. A
bobbing goblin. The hank and the quill of our
hungry fate. Escape that. We both think we will.

Imagine the beetle imagining the
wasp imagining what would be involved in
keeping a diary. I should have risked more. Done
nothing. Taken half, maybe. Never the whole
bake. But, it's a fact, no peas would then grow in
the field. They were unable to make butter,
or cheese. And that was it. A fly – always the
same fly? In summer weather it would shuttle
through the glints and darkness looming in her room.
Far too familiar, they said. Doubtless a
part of her repertoire. Some point of view, some
plenitude and cogency. Really? Nonplussed
on the glass, it knocks against the white outside.
It taps. His angry finger nail. Tap, tap. Some
privy agony? Eleven women, all
acquitted, and, it seemed to me, believing
nothing of the witchery! He sat up straight
as if the sky were resting on his head. The
wasp reads on. The beetle rips up what is read.

The beetle believes that you are watching it.
It lifts its chin, looks at you, and gets ready
to unsheathe its wings. The fascination of
a magician is ever by the eye and
to the heart. Mine aches. Dread hunts my ground as a
tiger beetle, reeves my quiet as a wasp.
I learn their manners and disguise myself as
them. But their movements figure out themselves. They
never choke on cake. It's a mistake to wish
that they could speak. They pass on this and that. Most
of this kind do take to the air at once, not
saying a word. And he cheerfully greeted
the more sensational testimony, with
the remark that he knew of no law against
flying. Staggered, they went out into the day.
Blind. Reeling with freedom. Who cares what they thought
that they thought that they thought? All such repertoires
are put to bed. The blanket design was an
old one, easy to pick out, worn to a thread.

Blues for Titania

The beetle runs into the future. He takes
to his heels in an action so frantic its
flicker seems to possess the slowness of deep
water. He has been green. He will be so yet.
His memory ripples emeralds. The wasp
takes it easy. She unpicks her fabric of
yellow and black, which slips from her fingers to
land in the past, loop-holed, lacy, tossed off on
the wing. The beetle is needled right through on
one string. He peels a strip as he packs a shelf.
He is thrilling the grass, and whatever it
means, it is radiantly green like himself. Thus
he will invest again and again in that
same flashy suit. The wasp has forgotten her
costume, but proves herself wise to the ways of
the sun, which are pat on her back. She drops a
curtsy, blows a kiss, and somersaults over
the beetle's attack. Lost moments swill round in
the shallows, until they can stick there and stack.

The beetle swears it's a set-up job. Follow
your mouth. Swallow tomorrow. Borrow and bet.
Rivet your eyes on the road, and do what you
said. You run through the beetles you have been, and
insist there are more of the same up ahead.
The wasp says goodbye to those she has never
met. She swirls down to just touch the track, so that
she definitely indicates her shadow,
a generous fellow, who has come on his
own, to join in. He's an item. And now he's
close kin. She gives him a hug. Then that's her in
mid-air and she's left him. He's a scoundrel, who
dodges about and grows dim. Neglected. The
necklace has snapped. Scramble for beads. Some of them
still roll and sparkle, prickling the gorse and the
stamens of the bittersweet. This will be the
best place for muttering nonsense. We could meet
anywhere in the wood. Tired in the hawthorn
brake. Tricked by the thick vegetation. Gutted.

A snatch at the clasp and a curse as our prayers
scatter. One of them comes to a stop by a
dazzling white stone. Others tag darker places.
So be it. Snipe lie near small pools, to hide in
their glare. Purple orchids are smuts in the dusk.
A wasp is humming as it investigates
the gravelly foreground, where no gods squat, but
someone pictured an overturned goblet. The
stub of a tree with a kingfisher on it.
Cybele carefully holds up a quince. Now
specialist theatres are opening all
along the hedge. Sparrows adopt passionate
poses in each of them. Detail is so sharp
and so minute that the total form suggests
infinity. Everything. Wincing. Oh, but
thereby, it seems to me, there is infinite
loneliness. Such tons of shingle. If I find
my feet in it, I will walk up and down and
sing, that they shall hear that I am not afraid.

The beetle straightens his jacket to confirm
an initial conception. After all there
are not many cores. The car doors slam behind
his shoulders and he pulls away into the
best, fast synthesis that there is, blazing down
the mid-line, the Roman Street, his heart in his
horn. The wasps and moths and feathers are riff-raff
off the verge. Stuff for his buffet. And isn't
Isis Demeter? No mysteries in here.
It's me, hands on the wheel, and capable of
brilliant wristy brushwork, if I rouse out
my conceit across the blur of foliage.
But. Who knows what monsters were revered by the
Egyptians? We must not boast or palter. Don't
rush the sense, or stagger if it's true. Ask me
not what. The duke has dined. Three layers of the
lapis, mixed with white lead. The last translucent
glaze, and no golden scumble. Cool and intense.
Guaranteed to be the bluest of the blue.

My Moth: My Song

It goes on. Hawk moths stammer in front of
the red valerian. These words, floated
in the silence, by myself, hover close
to my thoughts. The thoughts themselves almost were
words. I think they were. I think they did. How
close is close? What colour were the moths?
There was some orange on them, and the words
were white as water. Sometimes they referred
to orange. It is difficult to say,
for instance, what it is like to hold a
field mouse in your hand. It is exactly
brown, is it? But other people's words come
yammering about. You have to clutch your
own, inside your hand, where something seems to
prickle like water. You make decisions.
You don't experience them. Metaphors
are only other mice. This morning there
were other butterflies. Green hairstreaks. Two
kinds of swallowtails, flat out in hot sun.
Linnaeus bedevilled them with Homer.
A battle filled with butterflies. No red
thorax, so he said, means that these are Greeks.
Achivi. Pectore incruento.
Pat as a kiss, one settles, unnoticed,
on the rim of Nestor's chariot. It
flicks open to the page that you looked for.
Pectus maculis sanguineis. These
are Trojans who have wounded Machaon.
And Nestor tapped his horses with his whip.
Pick up our surgeon, Machaon, and drive
him to the hollow ships. Papilio
machaon. The red valerian is
a city. But it's hard to character
the whelk and drift of waves. Their eyebrows flash
metallic green. Those hairstreaks. Sometimes a
shape will follow you all day, through thickets,
disturbing the names, old indications,
the sort of education where the wit
of man is hard put to it to devise
more names. Callophrys. Beautiful eyebrows

in the bramble. Rubus. Hairstreak. Hawkmoth.
Macroglossum. Big tongues in the bedstraw.
Stellatarum. Starry, starry things. You
can be hooked all day on a dab of song.
Suddenly, in the shadow of a street,
a symbol is a face held out to you,
and close enough to have immediate
significance. I will think a little
promise for you. I will wrap your cap of
ferret-skin inside your wolf pelt. I will
dump them in the tamarisk bush, till I
come back, when tonight is young, around the
corner of the not so far away, to
find, held out to me, as I expected,
waiting to be tasted, certain spoils to
make it worth my while to uncoil my tongue.

Cash Point

Took a turn or
two across a plot
of May, to where
he saw wild thyme,
some clustered oxlips,
bunches of riviniana
violets

And, the way Adam
put it, their bodies seemed
incorporate with their
names. Cobwebs, sticky
on cut fingers. Tongues
caught up in the sweet
lexemes.

So, speaking leaves, he
said, 'Commend me to
this Mistress Squash, your
mother. Drive me together
all you can gather. The
stars can't be so far
away.'

Bring me that fellow called
Hay. Uncork a bottle of
smoke. Help the old lady
out of the bush. Hee
haw, when the cart has
passed and straws still glint
on some snags in the hedge.

Close your eyes and make
a mum with your mouth
shut. Just so. Now
look. The stanza is a
born dancer, out on
the green. Tongs and
bones in your good ear.

The notation is numinous.
Some patient gentleman with
the beak of an ibis is
writing it up, in case
any honey leaks from
a bee's thigh, or a hip
verb.

Bosky. The occult
semiosis of the forest.
A l'ombra d'un bel
faggio, where you dip
into syllables and
emerge stringing
pearls.

What had you in mind?
Red sienna? The fur
of a lappet? The purpling
tips of its wings? Or
this little chap, nodding,
perhaps, and wringing
his hands?

With your last twitch you can
point at the letters that make up
the spell. Too late to explain.
You are trained to assume
the soft applause of the Latin,
levis and *labi,* as you ask for
a wind to ripple the carpet.

Freeze and scream. You ragged
devil! He erupts in a bray and
glares with what might be
recognition. Asshead. Dolt.
Blunderer. O monstrous! O
Thisbe! Only thine! Only
a ninny!

But we are not on
stage, so that might be
the magus, Agrippa Von
Nettesheim, approaching
the hole in the wall,
with nothing to suggest we
should have his number.

Take a map. Park the car.
Undo your napkin in the
moonlight under the Duke's
Oak. Sort it. Pace it out. You
don't need ribbons on your
pumps. Just a note on the key
signs and an almanack.

'What it means
is not what it
refers to,' grumbled
Flute, rubbing the
stubble of his
orange-tawny
beard.

Kiss the rubric or the prayer.
Kiss your stipend till its
corners chink. Kiss the taste
of a freckle, or what the cow
slopped into the rough-cast.
Kiss lime. Kiss hair. Whatever
you think is not my lips.

Shadows cascade
down bales on
wagons which pass
away under trees,
and I swear that
they are fluent
enough.

Touchstone

Aquinas was wrong.
Science and religion are
not continuous. Thus:
the late robin in the
dark garden. A gift,

a lock, a wedge, an
order or a wistfulness.
A real bird in actual
space. And matter
constitutes the laws

allowing notes from a
perch on the line-post.
The head cocks, which seems
astute. Then the further
limits of our being plunge

back across the forty feet
into the hedge. You can recall
the flutter in your empty
ear. The bustle of the feathers
in your ear. Their brief mandamus.

Augustine was right.
There was no 'before'. The world
set off with time, not into it.
Accompanied by dusk the
further phrases sing out

off the line-post, melodic,
desultory, sweet snatches at
masks, small personal cheers,
most of your education for
these years. This grass and dusty

hawthorn and this ten o'clock
to float you home. Blue thistles
go to white. Magenta lychnis
blackens. A dragonfly is
allocated extra minutes to

astound the moths with vehement
flaunt-a-flaunt of possibilities. The
slight rustle of everything
immediate. Nothing here
is clandestine.

Descartes was wrong.
The decision to sing is
the first note of the song. It
discovers the bird there on
the line-post, as it is

already being sung. The
quick flexing of the legs is
unexpected. There is no
estimation of the hawthorn
and its forty feet away. White

thistles are what blinked.
Before it took a breath, the
robin was caught out in
what it saw, and what
it had to say. A touching

welladay? Not so. It was the
atoms of the August evening,
instantly genuine, distancing
themselves or perhaps
less torn apart.

Kepler was wrong to
talk of forces as if they
were things. Here they are
generated by the robin
which turns, now, to the north to

power a strict, ticking call in
that direction. The dragonfly
flays molecules along the hedge.
Nothing is mystic. The lure
is obvious and the bite is

a delight. What else is capable of
this spirit of alarm, together
with direct appraisal of the
autumn and the opportunities
of this very moment on the stock?

It has to be a material fool.
His warranty tempts me back
to see if I can find some record
of the magenta and the blue
which must be kept there.

Brute Conflict

It could be this. It could
be brute conflict. It could
be that I want to count
because I do not want
to count. The counter-wish
is wished to normalise
confusion. To desire.
To notice the absence
of the stars. Regretting
it. Glad that they have gone.
To calculate without
desires, so the pebbles
vanish when it comes to
calculation. Desire
for pebbles. The placid
images of shape and
weight. The cheerful pebbles.
The joy of having too
few fingers for the stars.
Abandon the trip to
the beach. Pebbles are so
much like pebbles that they
look back at you. Their gaze
rests upon you. You are
a disappointment to
yourself. What sort of a
laugh was that which you gave
to the night sky? Belief
is in this or that, but
you want horned poppies and
sums done without pictures.
You are quick to deny
your heart, but the leaves clasp
the stems and the seed pods
divert you with ribald
gestures. Four or five toys
remain on the table.
All small. None of them is
mechanical. Each has
come out of your secret

drawer. He could call down the
stars. He used anything
as an imprecation.
'You plate!' he swore. 'You lamp!
You towel!' But often
he saw a surge take up
the cobbles, jingle them,
then put them into place.
Often. Often. The same
rubbed round bodies of the
stones. Hit after hit. The
thorough hammering. No
cutlery. Brute conflict
and a restful nonsense.
Now five thousand starlings
no one ever counted
have settled in the reeds.

Skrymir's Glove

This morning in November in the bar
of the Angel there is an open fire.
I tell you this so you imagine it
as though the bar in the Angel were a
place that has been given to itself, full
of itself, filled with the things there are in
here, such as the fire. Not the words but the
flames. This is quite possible though you know
that what you have of it, its hum and pop,
could not be prior to the poem. You
don't take shelter in the darkness and the
cold of open countryside which, in the
morning, will turn out to be inside the
giant's glove. You sit down at a table
by the window where you can feel the flames,
take off your gloves, wait for Louise, who comes
through doors into such places, those given
to themselves. You still enjoy the way she
does, and here she is. Grey eyes. Black hair. Go
for the gloves. Fashioned by trolls, the food is
tied up in impenetrable iron.
The cat is stuck into the shape of sleep
and can't be levered off the floor. Your tongue
proves chocolate dust on cappuccino
froth. It's all as heavy and as hard as
that. But it holds good. There is some truth in
every bit of it. Louise can help, things
on her mind, her fingers lost around the
coffee cup. The good spectators will now
imagine someone facing her across
the table, where otherwise there would be
empty space. Someone is called to work on
a complete Louise, lever her off the
floor, fix her in iron, put her amongst
grey eyes, black hair, and seat her opposite.
That will be me, facing Louise, feeling
the fire inside the Angel bar, inside
the giant's glove, the window to my left.
I will arrive precisely when Louise
picks up her cup, touches the iron, wakes

the terrific cat, and both of us are
given to ourselves, together with trolls,
perhaps, and incredible November.

At Sotterley

Caravaggio raises Lazarus
on the Messina canvas
in Room Four, where they squiny
at the light that comes across
from behind Christ. Maybe they
think it is a snap of sun,
outside the cave, in March, in
Bethany.

        I walk, in March,
in fields, at Sotterley, and
look everywhere to see the
colour of the paint. Mars black,
iron oxide, chlorinated
copper phthalocyanine.
Green and grey and sepia
on the trunks of oaks. So this
is Martha's light, being left
to serve things as it can. The
work is in the kitchen.

            My
day was spent in walking through
the gardens at Notre Dame.
I saw his eyes were shining,
then I guessed that he had seen
someone behind me that he
came to meet. The glow of his
face is what I won't forget.

It's Lent. Unexpectedly
the oak trunks are caught cobalt
green.

        Martha is cooking and
nobody asked her what there
was to eat.

                    Ticket holders
like to think Room Four is the
dark cave where they get close to
actors they can recognise.
Back in Room One, this was the
man who grasped the table and
boggled with the shock. Which of
them is Caravaggio?
He and his friends are pulling
all the faces.

            If I had
seen his wife and child before
I saw his happiness, his
face would not have struck me so.

A truth to content you. In
the shape of a jug. The jug
be my judge. I drink in it
so the cold water quenches
my rascal. I pull myself
together, gulping down the
lonely Martha. I grasp the
table. Here comes a long draught
of my small, stale, icy beer.

A family behind me
are whispering about the
colours, in a language I
don't recognise. They come from
a country whose pictures are
like none in this gallery.
None that I have ever seen.

These characters have been told
to pick the jug up off the
table as they would do if
they were picking up a jug.

I leave a perfect heel print
on a molehill. Green lips lick.
These touchy chemicals have
no self control.

                    Warm it with
your ice-cold commentary.

I see the brushwork and I
read it back into the far,
well-swept corners of her floor,
the perspective of her path,
the Shrove-tide overcast she
glances at outside. One way
or another, if you are
a realist, you can do
no more.

                    This is Emilia,
twelve months old and waving to
the Christ Child in the Titian.

The brush calls your attention
to the jaw, to both lips, to
the nostril, the eyelid and
the smooth bulge under the brow.
Six strokes of his post-Roman
manner, reciprocating
with what looked like the truth in
Sicily. Turn round and be
in Bethany. Slow down and,
lost in a stand of oaks, there
is a woman with a broom.

They do not know which way to
look, and miss the hands in the
air above them. That will be
Mary who dares not touch her
brother's head in case it costs
the love of love. They can't see
that, either. They twist into
the lighting from stage right. I
can't hear what they say, but now,
I guess, they shout for help from Sotterley.

The Bellini in San Giovanni Crisostomo

It's curfew, and I do my turn
around the valley, settling down
outposts of mine, the little, far-
flung castles, Roche this and Rocca
that. And 'Check,' I say, and 'Split,' and
'Cover up my fire.' I rouse my
sentinels under relict clouds,
happy with some altostratus
and a roll of rosy billows
processing off the peaks. I start
the spleenwort by the door, argue
small slips and petals which still snap
with love or hate although it is
so dark and late. I stipulate
which bits matter. White chips go in
grey spaces. But, gradually,
the old man's face becomes more than
it was. His profile is on the
sky above the mountains. Nor does
he look at me, but only at
his book. He veils his eye and sucks
his lip, as he considers what
is read. And so it starts to move.
The castles and the clouds and the
asplenium which I still make
out, splayed on the rock, are taking
their places in his head. He has
a mind for them. Together with
his library, his fig tree, the
ridge he sits on, the cinquefoil, the
other weeds in cracks, here he comes,
with screes and summits and summer
pastures in the gloaming at his
back. He edges forwards under
the perspective of the foreground
arch, between the pair of flanking
saints who are inside already,
standing on the marble floor. Each
thing he brings is sharp as a stone
which I discover as I shake

my shoe, and tip it out to hear
it click and patter to a stop.
There is no need to badger at
the garrison, trooping home for
supper. Recall your champions.
Inform the tower, the gable,
silk on a mitre, the paper
label tacked on the parapet,
that they can have one moment more
to be expensive. The moon picks
at the corner of the page. I
turn myself around to thank him,
the old man, the moon, Bellini,
hoping the next words he reads will
mention me, as someone waiting
in the nave, at twilight, here in
line fifty-seven, arrested
by green and rose. By rose and brown.

Birdwatching Poem

For Robert Stone

In the twigs, *contorta*, of the two trees
which the council has planted by the new
apartment block – eight waxwing, bibbed, masked and
crested. At first they were conclusive black
up there in silhouette, then they flourished
down in splendid grey and cinnamon, dashed
out with writs of zinc and red. The tails tipped
in gold. A hundred years ago, Mutzel
engraved them, posed in conifers and birch.
His foreground was the usual broken
branch. He sheathed this one in moss to show a
swampy place in Fenno-Scandia. Might
be witch-hair lichen. They came in Volume
Three, between the shrikes and thrushes. They don't
care where they come. Nor who is watching them.
March heat. The plastic gutters start to pop.
The birds drop to the cotoneaster.
Heads bob. A berry is held up in a
beak. They leave across the demolition
site. Now raise your hand if you think you saw
the grapes of Zeuxis. You've earned yourself an
All Day Breakfast at the café on the
disused airfield, sausages, mushrooms, beans
and bacon, toast, hash browns and two fried eggs.
There will be thirteen days of North Sea cold
and overcast. Next time, ten birds in white
tenacious light, clipped to that same bare tree,
all of their colours in unshakeable
positions. Say what you saw. Come to the
topic unrehearsed. The scratches in the
cave are nothing but a family of
snowy owls. The youth at Fayum forgot
he had big ears and that his mouth was still
somewhat tucked up as he imagined he
was dead. He felt how far it is. The nip
is in the small purse of his lip. It is
conclusive. Now it is flourishing in
his winter face. Now it has signed him. You

see that? And it is written so there is
nothing to translate. Mutzel, of course, saw
owls, and then a waxwing, holding a red
berry in its beak. Immediately
outside. Distance was there at once. There was
a disused airfield, people still working
in the café. Breakfast. Not far to seek.

Il Redentore

Eight hours out from Stansted then the
numbers can go handsome. The star
turn of eight between the six and
twelve. Unfluted columns. Whitewashed
walls. Corinthian acanthus
with volutes that spin up to trump
the tiers of leaves and clinch the horns
of abaci. In this calm light
complexity settles into
perfect focus. *Concinnitas.*
Correction hums. The length of smooth
grey architrave levels across
arrested foliage. Then comes
the creamy frieze, then, grey again,
the cornice. Hundreds of dentels
corrugate its strike. Loosed into
systems, other shadows of this
gentle afternoon lie upside
down on archivolts and cusps of
niches. Outside the clear glass of
the west door, the green canal puts
up a hand, and then another
further on, a second silver
hand, to show two corners of the
stone revetment, so that, from here
to here, there is *una certa
convenienza* in all the
body, *tutto bello.* Six is
to eight as eight is to twelve. You
step back into creamy heat and
your eyes go grey. Nine is to six
as six is to three. The ticket
for the vaporetto is where
it ought to be, tucked into this
top pocket. Eight is to four as
four is to two. *Valido.* The
day and hour. Both have come true. Your
tongue is held between your teeth. To
order and explore. Some certain
people stand where you can count on

finding them. A son you came to
meet is in the salizada,
by his shadow, rustling paper
as he checks the name that should be
by the bell. You had him timed for
half-past eight. It's twenty-five to
nine, and, *tutto bello*, here are
the hundred good hellos, ready
to say. More shadows follow files
of clouds that run straight off the coast
of Sussex. The warm ground raised them,
thermals which condensed in puffs to
be picked off by wind that took them
out to sea. Neurons move in the
mind, *psi*, *phi* and *omega*, Freud
said. Their quantities determine
their different directions. Well.
Tutto bello. And your eyes go
grey. A woman, dressed in black, moves
in the nave, diminutive. A
woman with white hair has entered
and is tracking east. The woman
carries stick and prayer book. Eros
binds, Freud says. The woman bears her
body stiff and black, bound in the
transparent air. She has strapped her
body to its backbone and she
keeps it up and going with a
stutter of short steps. Her aim is
to preserve the long walk up the
nave, and so she is a poet
and Palladio. Leg after
leg into the second pew. She
climbs in with her hundred legs and
bends her head. In retrospect I
can ignore the facts and see her
triumph there, a dark acanthus.

The Wall Tomb of Giacomo Surian

Magnificent eagles heave and
whap their wings on Bruni's tomb. On
Zanetti's is a *feston* where
an eagle thrashes. She spreads and
screams. In Santo Stefano, in
half-light from the door, two griffins
sit under the sarcophagus.

Tackle the right-hand one. Try some
account analysis and a
repertory grid. Tell him you
know what he intends. Pretend that
people can make choices. Treat him
as if he did. Ascribe to him
a moral sensibility.

Flatter him as if you nursed a
dangerous baby, as if you
were a widow with a sulky
cat. Invest him with panoply
which is appropriate. Curse him
for looking like a buzzard, with
no feathers on his armoured legs.

He heard you coming in, and ducked
and swung his head towards the door.
His beak is opening, and the
tongue inside lies flat. Nictating
membranes flicker up his eyes and
he will snap. The gimlet nostrils
have been drilled below a skinny
frill that serves him as a cere. And
he will snap. He will now lunge and
snap.

His talons are grabbling on
the modillion, which has three
crisped seed-pods cut on it, just as
it should. You twist his tail until
it pops into a tuft of flame.

Alongside him, a little fat
boy leans, inscrutable, against
the ear of the inscription plaque,
and he holds up a torch of *Hope*
or *Life*. Another time, he will
get round to some intentions for
himself.

Outside the door crouches
a woman. She holds a plastic
cup, and is the beggar on the
steps. I'm pretty sure that this is
her across the city, later
on today, outside the Billa
supermarket, with her mother,
both carrying two shopping bags.

Deep into these transactions with
myself I send for words that will
extend some eagles on the wind.

Achilles

One is seldom directed by way of
an indigo gate. A life is plunged in
colours, saturations, shades, tints, hues. One
screws one's eyes up. A mediaeval list
of inks confuses *fuscum pulverum*
with azure from the Mines of Solomon.
Who knows what perse is? Days lose themselves in
pandia omnia and dip away
between the pinks and blues. But then there is
alizarin which sometimes jumps from the
old leaves. And turquoise is a stone dropped near
the gamboge fence. Who did not notice those?

And shapes. The tree. It shows what one could call
constraint. It bursts through rocks in calluses
that clog into a lump with several
branches lunging out of it, one knot-hole
and a stump. The thing has corners to it,
pockets, ledges, wedges, all chocked in with
lichen on them, found out by the sun that
stabs down from the right, detecting olive
green.

In sixteen-thirty-three, when she was
twenty-five, on a creamy marble slab
in the south aisle, they drew Elizabeth
Havers. Did she have time to walk out past
a red house? Choose a brush? Paint a picket
white? Step on by? Turn round, look back, and shout
that she could see what it might mean? That that
was the place where she had been? She is a
whisper. Smoke and cream. What had she really
seen? She rolls her eyes and wears her shroud so
that it does not cover her lace cuff.

The
kylix has been cracked. The mend in it spoils
his cheek-piece and his mouth, but there is still
his eye, under the helmet's rim, as he
stabs her from the right. She reaches up to
touch his chin. BC. Four-sixty. Killing
Penthesileia. It is his last and
only chance to stare at her. He does so
and he falls in love. Or is it lust or
scorn? Furious concentration? Don't call
it blue. Not blue. The gate is indigo.

She is engraved on her stone slab. The aisle
window moves its print onto her face. It
stresses her lips, almost rubbed out, and the
scoring of her thick curls. Her tear-ducts. The
look she is giving to her left, which might
be sad because she is remembering
what? Ten minutes of after-glow, when white
campion seemed distilled against grey grass,
the poppy in the crop, alight, red for
itself, and she stood stupefied by that,
hoping the hero had not seen her yet.

If she had lived she would be sixty-five.
Sir Isaac Newton, in a dark room, pins
his paper, sets his prism twenty-two
feet off, and asks a friend, who has not thought
about the harmony of tones in sounds
and colours, if he will mark each hue at
its most brisk and full. If he can, also,
postulate, along the insensible
gradation, the edges of the seven.
Where blue ends. Where the violet begins.
The pencil in hand. The hand and pencil
are suddenly intensely indigo.

The gate is indigo, but when they give
directions people call it blue. To lose
the way is to remember something of
the stump. But can anyone be ready
for the moment when the dusk ignites the
poppy? Or accept that the spectral hand
is his? That it's he must keep the pencil
steady? Maybe everyone is dazzled
here by simultaneous death and love?

This morning in
the pool at

Lime Kiln Sluice
a heron wades and

his deliberations are
proposing ripples

which reflect on
him, run silver

collars up his
neck, chuckle his

chin, then thin to
sting the silence

where he points
his beak.

His round
and rigid eye.

Perhaps he knows
he is caressed.

Spoken Soon

Under superb
trees

wandering with a
sleepy wish

the shadow of my head
pre-empts me

full of its thought and
nonchalant, travelling

through trees. Thick
and fast examples

crowd the brink. I say
Enchanter's nightshade.

Yellow pimpernel.
Some smaller sort of

willow-herb. White. White
and magenta. Spick

and span and strawberry.
The sprangle of the tree.

The aspen as it takes possession
of the notebook. No one

is buried in the sand. Enough.
I say a pile of logs.

Hornbeam and ash.
The bark almost intact,

polished or matt. Hot
in the glade. Bright

beetles nominate.
Thanasimus. Clytus.

The paragons run every way
in red and black and gold.

Enough, I say. Your
faces in the evening.

Spoke and spoon. Enough
the bowls of milk and

strawberries.
Mikael sleeping.

Joff with his lyre,
Naima recognising me

across the water. My
bravery is carried down

a cart-road by the summer
breeze, on the dividing light,

at the direction of a cloud and
nonchalantly balancing her wave.